I0426170

Kalaupapa National Historical Park (KALA) Marine Fish Monitoring Program Annual Status Report for 2008

Pacific Island Network

Natural Resource Data Series NPS/PACN/NRDS—2012/283

Kalaupapa National Historical Park (KALA) Marine Fish Monitoring Program Annual Status Report for 2008

Pacific Island Network

Natural Resource Data Series NPS/PACN/NRDS—2012/283

Eric Brown, Kimberly Tice
National Park Service
Kalaupapa National Historical Park
P.O. Box 2222
Kalaupapa, Moloka'i, Hawai'i 96742

Tahzay Jones
National Park Service
Inventory and Monitoring Program, Pacific Island Network
Hawai'i Volcanoes National Park
P.O. Box 52
Hawai'i National Park, Hawai'i 96718-0052

April 2012

U.S. Department of the Interior
National Park Service
Natural Resource Stewardship and Science
Fort Collins, Colorado

The National Park Service, Natural Resource Stewardship and Science office in Fort Collins, Colorado publishes a range of reports that address natural resource topics of interest and applicability to a broad audience in the National Park Service and others in natural resource management, including scientists, conservation and environmental constituencies, and the public.

The Natural Resource Data Series is intended for the timely release of basic data sets and data summaries. Care has been taken to assure accuracy of raw data values, but a thorough analysis and interpretation of the data has not been completed. Consequently, the initial analyses of data in this report are provisional and subject to change.

All manuscripts in the series receive the appropriate level of peer review to ensure that the information is scientifically credible, technically accurate, appropriately written for the intended audience, and designed and published in a professional manner.

Data in this report were collected and analyzed using methods based on established, peer-reviewed protocols and were analyzed and interpreted within the guidelines of the protocols.

Views, statements, findings, conclusions, recommendations, and data in this report do not necessarily reflect views and policies of the National Park Service, U.S. Department of the Interior. Mention of trade names or commercial products does not constitute endorsement or recommendation for use by the U.S. Government.

This report is available from NPS Inventory and Monitoring, Pacific Island Network (http://science.nature.nps.gov/im/units/pacn/index.cfm) and the Natural Resource Publications Management website (http://www.nature.nps.gov/publications/nrpm/).

Please cite this publication as:

Brown, E., K. Tice, and T. Jones. 2012. Kalaupapa National Historical Park (KALA) marine fish monitoring program annual report for 2008: Pacific Island Network. Natural Resource Data Series NPS/PACN/NRDS—2012/283. National Park Service, Fort Collins, Colorado.

NPS 491/113552, April 2012

Contents

Figures

Tables

Executive Summary

Kalaupapa National Historical Park (KALA) is located on the north shore of the island of Moloka'i and encompasses a wide variety of habitats from submerged marine resources to lowland coastal, mesic, and rainforest habitats as well as three offshore islands. The marine boundary of the park extends a quarter mile offshore around the park shoreline and encompasses approximately 2,000 acres.

The objective of the marine fish monitoring protocol is to annually determine the density and size of reef fishes at sites randomly selected on hard substrata in an isobath between the 10 and 20 m depths (Brown et al. 2011). From 2006-2008, a total of 30 transects (sites) were sampled each year. A split panel sampling design was used with 15 transects randomly established at the onset as fixed or permanent transects. These fixed transects were surveyed in 2006 and will be continually surveyed on an annual basis. The remaining 15 temporary transects were randomly selected each year and surveyed only in that year. Data collection consisted of a visual count and size estimation of all fish within 25 x 5 m underwater belt transects. Scientific divers were used to conduct this non-destructive technique and focused on the diurnal or day-active fish species that were highly visible due to their typically bright coloration and generally large size. This report includes the status of the fish populations at all 30 transects in 2008 and trends at the fifteen fixed transects from 2006-2008.

In 2008:
- Fish species richness ranged from 12 to 38 species per transect (125 m^2). Species richness was lowest on the western shore, and highest along the eastern shore, of the Kalaupapa peninsula.
- The density of fish at all transects ranged from 360 to 4,944 fish/km^2 x 1,000. The lowest densities were found near the western boundary of the park and along the southwestern coast of the peninsula. The highest fish densities were concentrated near the northern tip of the peninsula.
- Fish biomass at almost all transects ranged between 14.5 and 608.0 metric tons/km^2. At Temporary Transect 10, however, which is located on the eastern coast of the peninsula, biomass was more than twice that observed at any other transect (1,299.8 metric tons/km^2).
- Fish diversity (H') ranged from 0.73 to 3.03. The highest diversity values were concentrated near the western boundary of the park.
- Secondary consumers accounted for 83% of the individual fish observed during surveys in 2008, while apex predators accounted for just 1%, with primary consumers making up the remaining 16%. In contrast, the relative biomass of secondary consumers was 42%, compared to 7% for apex predators and 51% for primary consumers.
- In terms of density, the secondary consumer *Chromis vanderbilti* was by far the most abundant species. It was more than eight times as abundant as the next two most common taxa in the park combined (the secondary consumer *Naso hexacanthus* and the primary consumer *Kyphosus* spp.). The bulk of the biomass, however, was accounted for by these two species.

Trends at the 15 fixed transects surveyed annually from 2006-2008 showed that:

- Mean fish species richness remained relatively stable at approximately 24 species per transect.
- Mean fish biomass remained relatively stable at approximately 158 mt/km^2.
- Mean fish diversity (H') remained relatively stable at approximately 2.
- Mean fish density showed a slight decrease in 2007, although the level in 2008 (approximately 1,744 fish/km^2 x 1,000) was back up near the 2006 level.

Acknowledgments

We would like to thank Randall Watanuki, other KALA staff, and all the volunteers at Kalaupapa National Historical Park for their continuing logistical support in collecting the data for this report. Financial assistance was provided by the Pacific Island Network Inventory and Monitoring Program. We could not have done the work without this support.

List of Terms and Acronyms

KALA: Kalaupapa National Historical Park

PACN: Pacific Island Network

Trophic groups: groups defined by nutritional habits and requirements

Introduction

Because of their importance ecologically, culturally and economically, it is critical that Pacific Island Network (PACN) parks have scientifically rigorous data on the current health and long-term trends of the marine fish communities within their boundaries. In most Pacific parks, coral reefs form an important component of the ecosystem, and have been compared to tropical rainforests in terms of their high species diversity and complexity of interactions (Connell 1978, Birkeland 1997). Within coral reefs, marine fish are one of the most visible resources and certainly the most exploited.

Kalaupapa National Historical Park (KALA) in the PACN is located in Hawai'i on the north shore of the island of Moloka'i, and encompasses a wide variety of habitats from submerged marine resources to lowland coastal, mesic, and rainforest habitats as well as three offshore islands (Figure 1). The park preserves and interprets the Kalaupapa settlement and Hansen's disease patients, but public visitation is restricted. The marine boundary of the park extends a quarter mile offshore around the park shoreline and encompasses approximately 2,000 acres. Significant marine resources include the presence of threatened (green sea turtle) and endangered (monk seal, humpback whale) species, high wave energy coral reef communities, and relatively healthy marine intertidal and fish resources. The most common species of hermatypic corals occur at KALA, but prevailing oceanographic conditions prevent coral reef formation. The intertidal areas consist of exposed basalt benches, low and high cliffs, basalt boulder and cobble beaches, sand beaches, and numerous tide pools that provide habitat for juvenile fish species. Upland development (including sedimentation and other runoff-associated issues) and overfishing (including from commercial fishing vessels) are significant anthropogenic factors affecting fish communities at KALA.

The initial source of information on fish assemblages at KALA is from Beets et al. (2010) who surveyed the reefs from 2004 to 2005. Their data on species richness, numerical density, biomass, and diversity was the first known study to document fish habitat utilization patterns within the park boundaries. Recently, Coles et al. (2008) surveyed the offshore islands in and around the park for unique fish species, numerical density levels, biomass, and diversity. Reef Environmental Education Foundation (REEF; www.reef.org) also has two sites on the north coast of Moloka'i that provide species checklist information in similar habitats.

The methodology to monitor coral reef fish has been developed over the past 25 years, resulting in several commonly used survey techniques (e.g., Bohnsack and Bannerot 1986, Rogers et al. 1994, English et al. 1997, Samoilys 1997, Sweatman et al. 1998, Atlantic and Gulf Rapid Reef Assessment 2000, Hill and Wilkinson 2004). The technique adopted for PACN consists of a visual count and size estimation of fish by scientific divers along underwater 25 m x 5 m belt transects (Brown et al. 2011). This non-destructive technique focuses on one major component of the coral reef fish community—the diurnal or day-active fish species that are highly visible due to their typically bright coloration and generally large size. These species are the most heavily targeted by local fishers. While the small, cryptic or nocturnal species contribute to biodiversity and may be of ecological or management importance, the additional effort and time required to sample nocturnal and cryptic fish is not usually feasible with available resources. The visual estimate of fish size is an important component of these surveys for several reasons. First, lengths allow a conversion from fish numbers to biomass by using established length-weight relationships. Second, lengths are often a useful indicator of fishing pressure or population dynamics, e.g., a trend of decreasing sizes may indicate overfishing, or recruitment year classes. Third, there is a strong positive correlation between fish size and fecundity (reproductive potential) which, along with recruitment success, is important in assessing ecological services provided by park fish stocks.

The purpose of this report was to document the status of the marine fish assemblage at KALA in 2008 and examine changes from 2006 to 2008. First, the status of the entire assemblage in 2008 was analyzed for species richness, density, biomass and diversity using spatial distribution maps. Second, the trophic composition of the entire assemblage in 2008 was examined for both density and biomass. Third, the top ten species in 2008 in terms of density and biomass were listed to examine specific components of the assemblage. Finally, trends in the entire assemblage from 2006-2008 were plotted for species richness, density, biomass, and diversity.

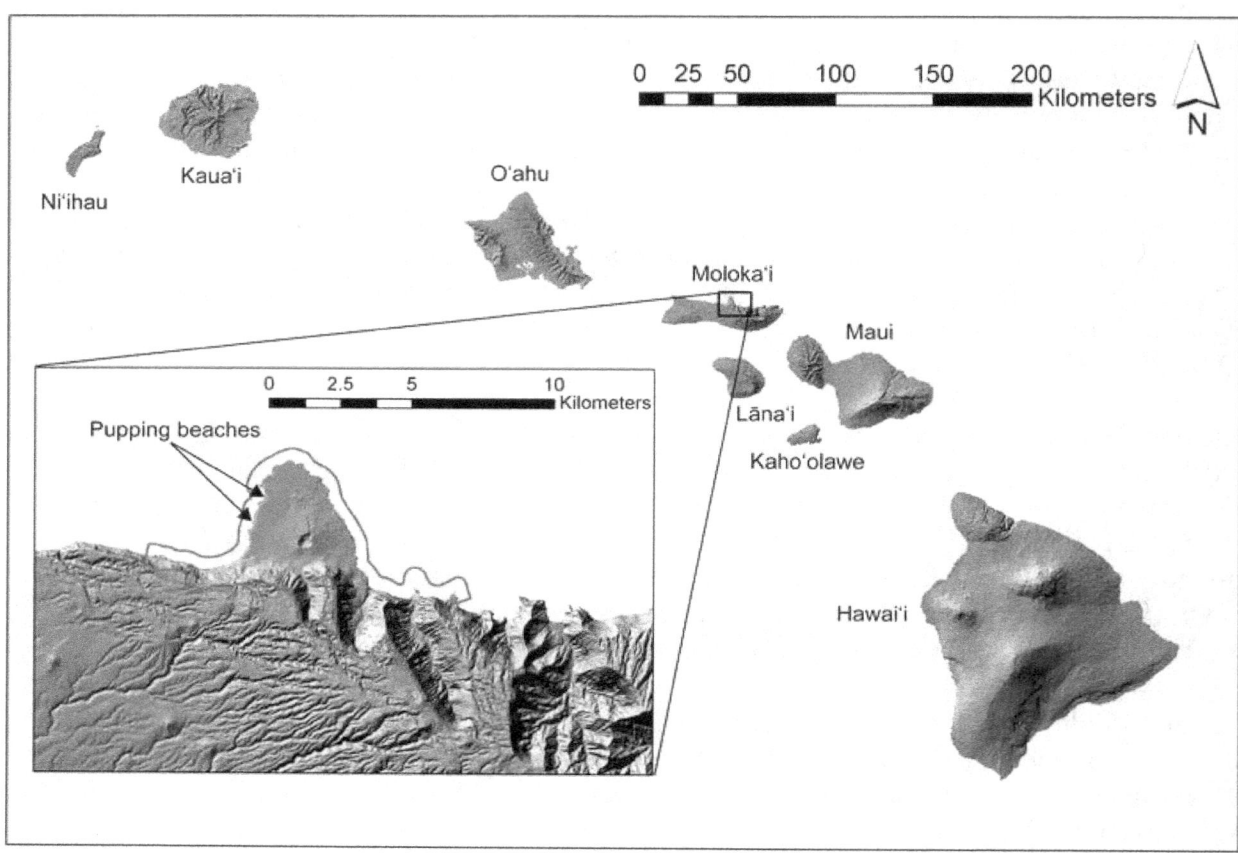

Figure 1. Map of the Main Hawaiian Islands showing Kalaupapa National Historical Park with the park boundary delineated as a red line in the inset.

Methods

Sampling Locations

A split panel design was used with 30 belt transects (25 m long x 5 m wide) sampled annually between 2006 and 2008. All transects were randomly selected using ArcMap® within the KALA sampling frame on hard bottom substrate in the depth zone between the 10-20 m isobaths (Figure 2). Fifteen fixed (permanent) transects were randomly selected at the onset of the monitoring program in 2006 and marked with stainless steel pins for relocation purposes. These sites were sampled every subsequent year. The remaining 15 temporary transects were randomly selected each year of monitoring and sampled only once. Transect locations were located in the field using a GPS unit.

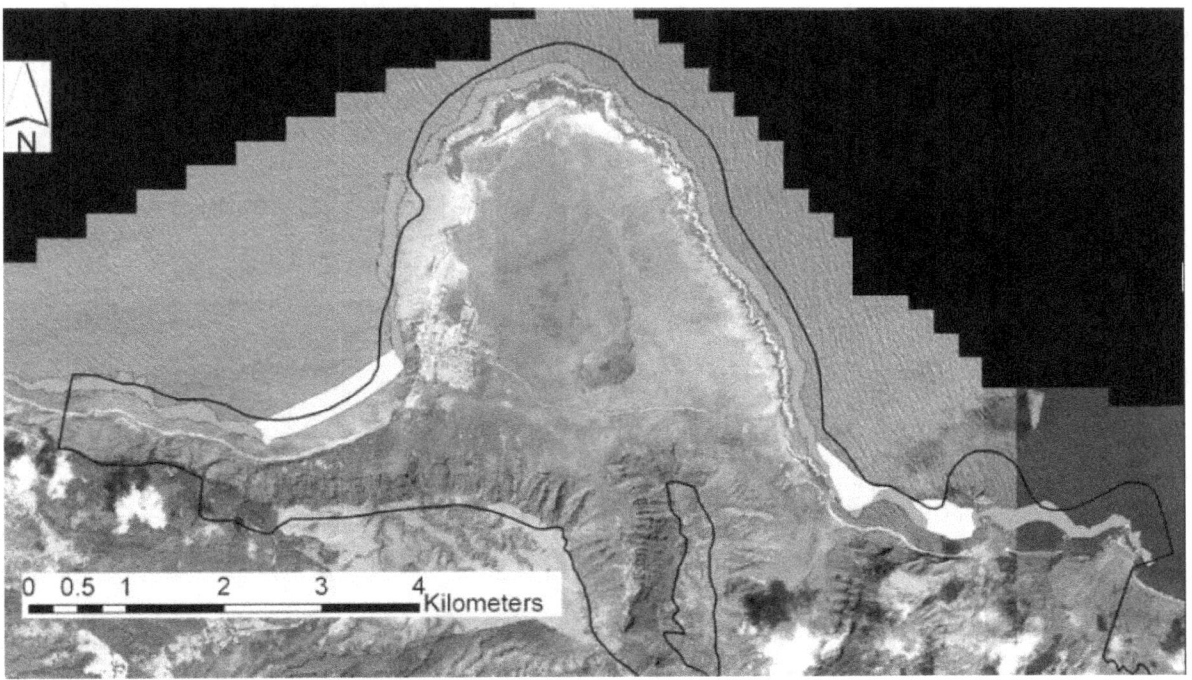

Figure 2. Light red polygons show sampling frame between 10 m and 20 m depth on hard bottom substrate at Kalaupapa National Historical Park. Sand habitat is shown by yellow polygons.

Survey Methods

Surveys occurred during the summer months from July through August. At each site, using SCUBA, the fish observer deployed a transect line along a constant depth contour which was typically parallel to shore. Locations, bearings, and depths of all 2008 transects are in Table 1. The observer counted and estimated the length (to the nearest centimeter) of all fish encountered along the distance of this transect. For this report, total length is used instead of standard length.

Data Analyses

Fish species richness for each transect was calculated by summing the number of different species observed per transect area (125 m^2).

Fish density at each transect was the total number of fish observed within each transect area of 125 m^2. This initial value was extrapolated to the number of fish per square kilometer (no./km^2) for display purposes and for comparison with other studies. To reduce the number of significant digits, fish densities represented in figures and tables are divided by 1,000, and need to be multiplied by 1,000 to get the actual density [(no./km^2) x 1,000].

Length estimates of fishes were converted to biomass using the following length-mass relationship derived for each species: Mass = a*(Standard Length)^b where a and b are species-specific constants for the allometric growth equation, standard length (SL) is in millimeters, and mass is in grams (Kulbicki et al. 1993, Friedlander et al. 2003). Total length was converted to standard length using conversion factors obtained from FishBase (www.fishbase.org). Length–mass fitting parameters were available for 150 species commonly observed on visual fish transects in Hawai'i from the Hawai'i Cooperative Fishery Research Unit (Friedlander et. al., 1997). This was supplemented with information from other published and web-based sources. In the cases where length–mass information did not exist for a given species, the parameters from similar bodied congeners are used. Biomass estimates for each transect were converted to metric tons per square kilometer (mt/km^2) to facilitate comparisons with other studies worldwide.

The Shannon index (H') was used to calculate species diversity within each transect using the following formula:

$$H' = -\sum_{i=1}^{S}(p_i \ln p_i)$$

where S is the total number of species and p_i is the frequency of the ith species in that transect.

To determine the trophic composition of the fish assemblage, each species was classified as a primary consumer, secondary consumer, or apex predator. Information on fish trophic group classifications was obtained from Friedlander et al. (1997), Fishbase, and other web-based sources.

Table 1. Metadata for Kalaupapa National Historical Park in 2008.

Year	Transect Type	Transect	UTM Zone	Datum	X (UTM)	Y (UTM)	Survey Date	Bearing (°)	Depth (m)	Chain_length (m)	Tape_length (m)	Rugosity
2008	Fixed	1	4N	NAD83	706010	2344139	7/21/2008	90.00	17.50	36.95	25.23	1.46
2008	Fixed	2	4N	NAD83	706258	2344036	7/22/2008	120.00	12.90	35.88	25.11	1.43
2008	Fixed	3	4N	NAD83	708983	2344924	8/27/2008	0.00	14.20	41.24	25.35	1.63
2008	Fixed	4	4N	NAD83	708894	2345511	7/22/2008	30.00	18.50	36.07	25.18	1.43
2008	Fixed	5	4N	NAD83	709266	2346429	7/23/2008	90.00	11.20	39.36	25.94	1.52
2008	Fixed	6	4N	NAD83	709377	2346496	7/22/2008	30.00	12.70	31.72	25.04	1.27
2008	Fixed	7	4N	NAD83	709481	2346801	7/23/2008	60.00	20.90	58.03	26.40	2.20
2008	Fixed	8	4N	NAD83	710816	2347337	8/19/2008	90.00	15.00	51.80	25.35	2.04
2008	Fixed	9	4N	NAD83	711136	2347201	8/19/2008	120.00	15.90	42.79	25.32	1.69
2008	Fixed	10	4N	NAD83	712308	2345598	8/27/2008	150.00	16.30	37.94	25.20	1.51
2008	Fixed	11	4N	NAD83	712922	2344752	8/26/2008	150.00	15.30	42.72	25.40	1.68
2008	Fixed	12	4N	NAD83	713052	2344465	8/26/2008	180.00	17.30	41.63	25.39	1.64
2008	Fixed	13	4N	NAD83	713059	2343922	8/26/2008	150.00	13.60	36.49	24.80	1.47
2008	Fixed	14	4N	NAD83	715830	2342575	8/20/2008	210.00	14.30	37.81	26.01	1.45
2008	Fixed	15	4N	NAD83	716364	2342586	8/20/2008	270.00	13.70	39.42	25.05	1.57
2008	Temporary	1	4N	NAD83	705033	2344186	7/21/2008	90.00	18.10	40.70	25.00	1.63
2008	Temporary	2	4N	NAD83	705851	2344092	7/21/2008	260.00	17.10	41.15	25.00	1.65
2008	Temporary	3	4N	NAD83	706212	2344125	7/22/2008	90.00	16.60	35.95	25.00	1.44
2008	Temporary	4	4N	NAD83	709070	2346188	7/22/2008	220.00	12.80	34.88	25.00	1.40
2008	Temporary	5	4N	NAD83	709502	2346743	7/23/2008	200.00	11.50	36.85	25.00	1.47
2008	Temporary	6	4N	NAD83	710135	2347282	8/25/2008	60.00	18.50	51.87	25.00	2.07
2008	Temporary	7	4N	NAD83	710344	2347265	8/25/2008	60.00	13.00	29.27	25.00	1.17
2008	Temporary	8	4N	NAD83	711587	2346816	8/20/2008	150.00	16.70	53.41	25.00	2.14
2008	Temporary	9	4N	NAD83	712088	2346409	8/19/2008	150.00	21.40	49.59	25.00	1.98
2008	Temporary	10	4N	NAD83	712302	2345677	8/27/2008	150.00	19.00	35.85	25.00	1.43
2008	Temporary	11	4N	NAD83	712590	2345211	8/26/2008	120.00	14.60	40.12	25.00	1.60
2008	Temporary	12	4N	NAD83	712710	2344981	8/26/2008	150.00	12.50	48.85	25.00	1.95
2009	Temporary	13	4N	NAD83	715193	2342722	7/14/2009	240.00	19.30	34.35	25.00	1.37
2009	Temporary	14	4N	NAD83	715769	2342583	7/14/2009	330.00	11.60	36.03	25.00	1.44
2009	Temporary	15	4N	NAD83	716181	2342574	7/14/2009	260.00	20.50	44.89	25.00	1.80

Results

Metadata

A total of fifteen fixed and fifteen temporary transects were surveyed at Kalaupapa National Historical Park in 2008 (Table 1). The survey time period spanned 38 days from July 21, 2008 to August 27, 2008 with 9 days of actual field time to conduct the surveys.

Status of Fish Assemblage Characteristics

Fish species richness ranged from 12 to 38 species per transect (125 m^2; Figure 3). Species richness was lowest on the western shore, and highest along the eastern shore, of the Kalaupapa peninsula.

The density of fish at all transects ranged from 360 to 4,944 fish/km^2 x 1,000 (Figure 4). The lowest densities were found near the western boundary of the park and along the southwestern coast of the peninsula. The highest fish densities were concentrated near the northern tip of the peninsula.

Fish biomass at almost all transects ranged between 14.5 and 608.0 metric tons/km^2 (Figure 5). At Temporary Transect 10, however, which is located on the eastern coast of the peninsula, biomass was more than twice that observed at any other transect (1,299.8 metric tons/km^2).

Fish diversity (H') ranged from 0.73 to 3.03 (Figure 6). The highest diversity values were concentrated near the western boundary of the park.

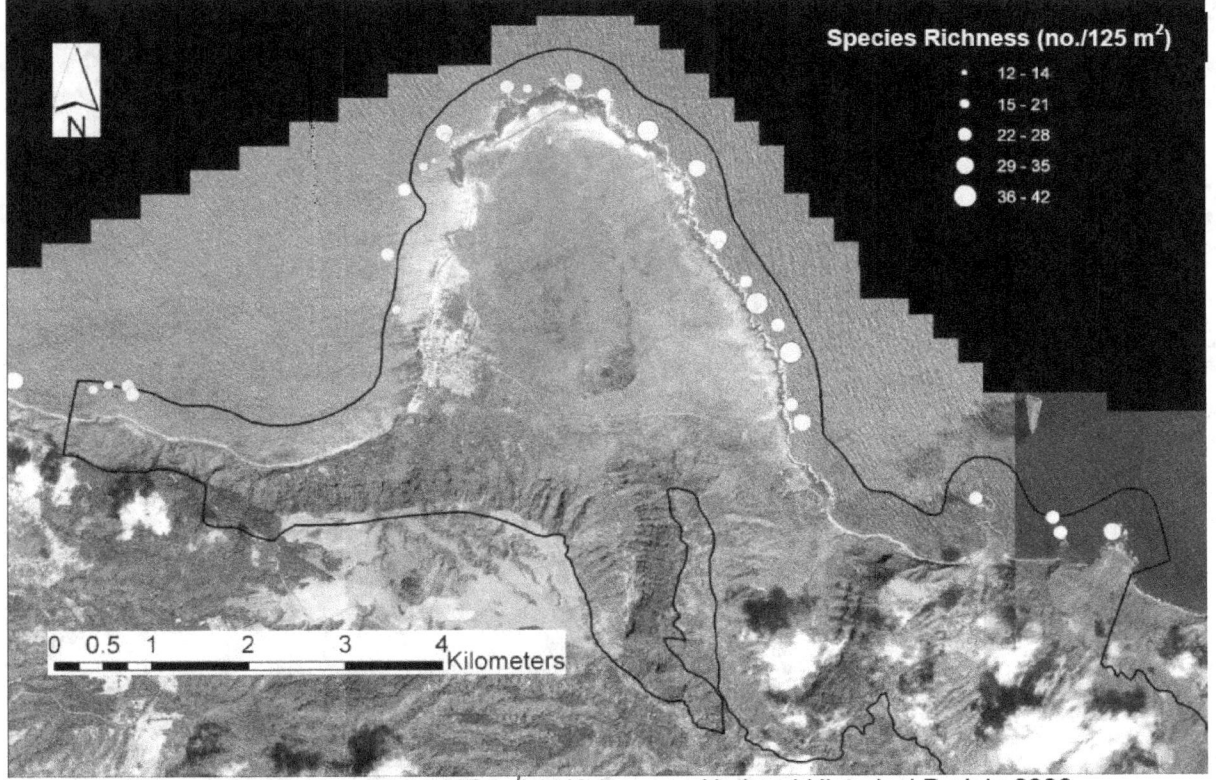

Figure 3. Fish species richness (no./125 m^2) at Kalaupapa National Historical Park in 2008.

7

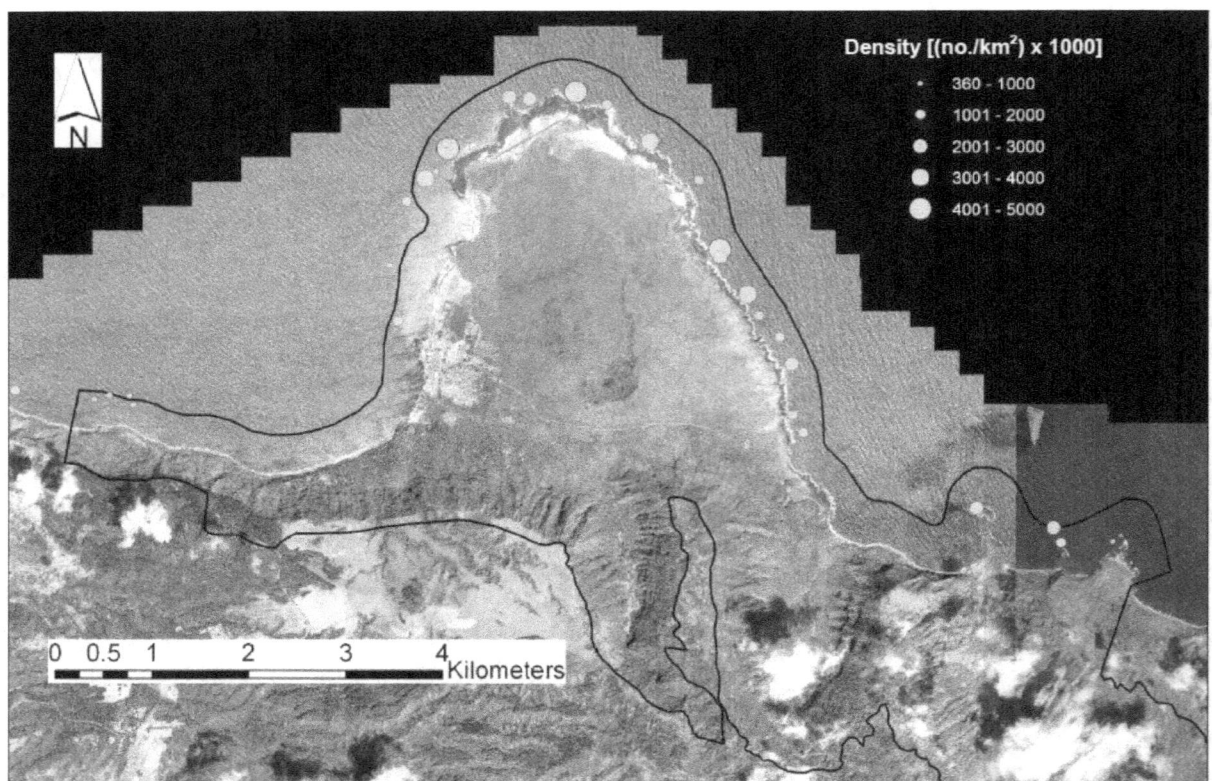

Figure 4. Fish density [(no./km^2) x 1000] at Kalaupapa National Historical Park in 2008.

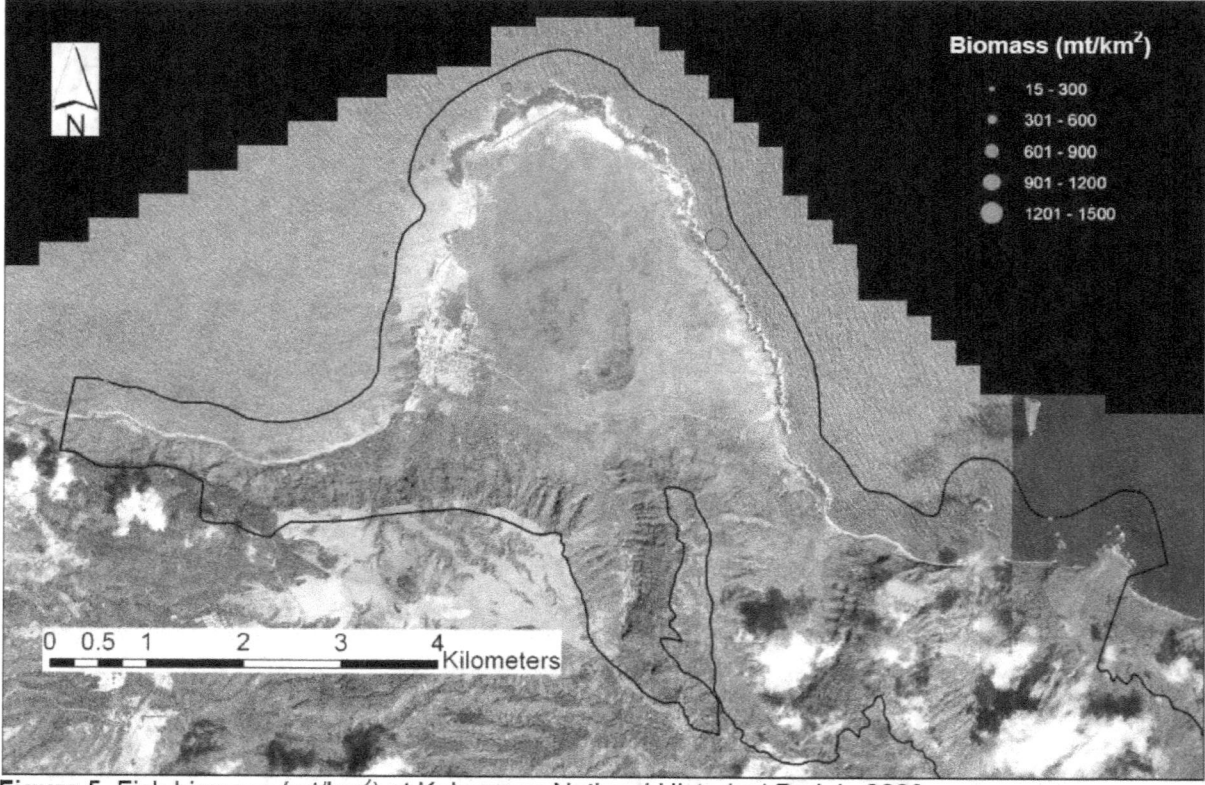

Figure 5. Fish biomass (mt/km^2) at Kalaupapa National Historical Park in 2008.

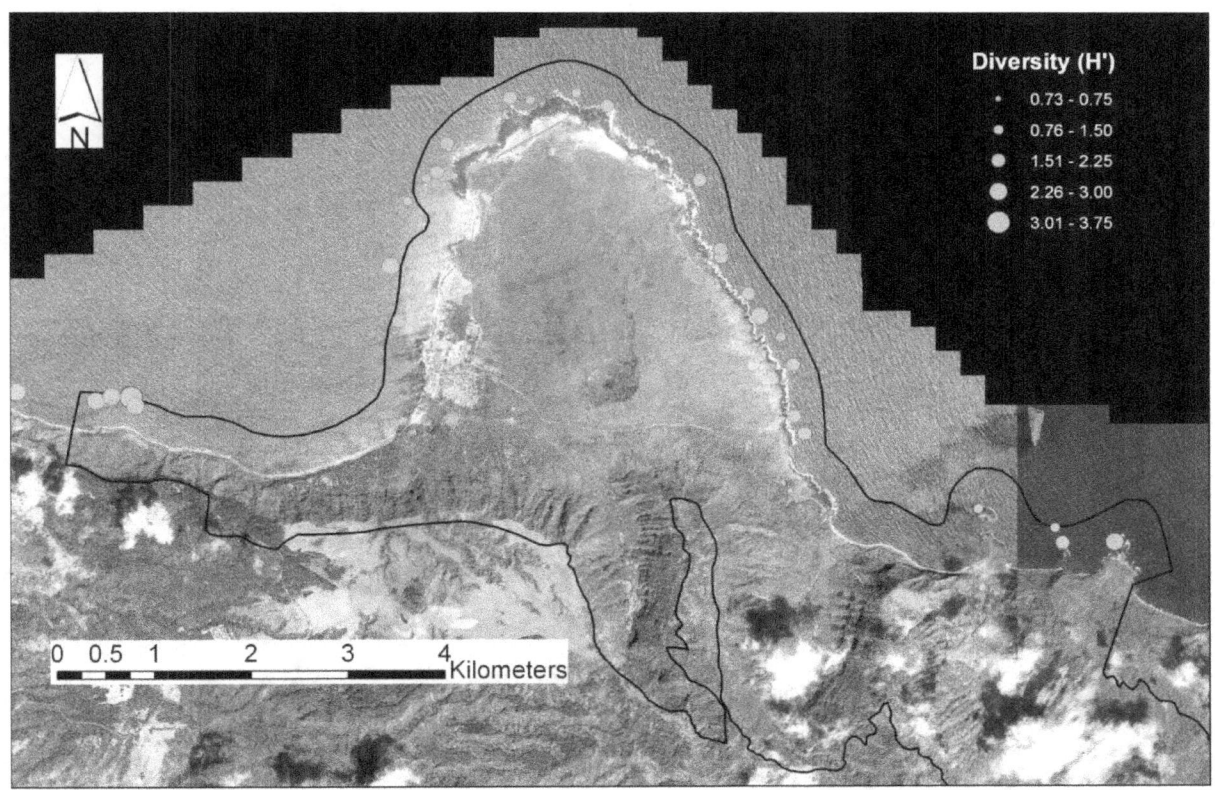

Figure 6. Fish diversity (H') at Kalaupapa National Historical Park in 2008.

Trophic Composition of the Fish Assemblage

Secondary consumers accounted for 83% of the fish density observed during surveys in 2008, while apex predators accounted for just 1%, with primary consumers making up the remaining 16% (Figure 7). In contrast, the relative biomass of secondary consumers was 42%, compared to 7% for apex predators and 51% for primary consumers (Figure 8).

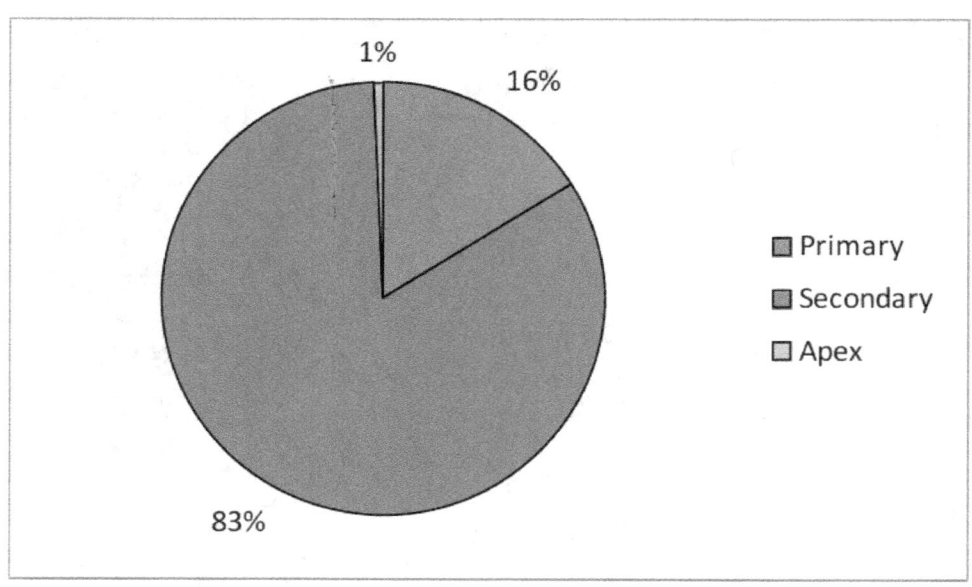

Figure 7. Relative density of fish consumer groups at Kalaupapa National Historical Park in 2008.

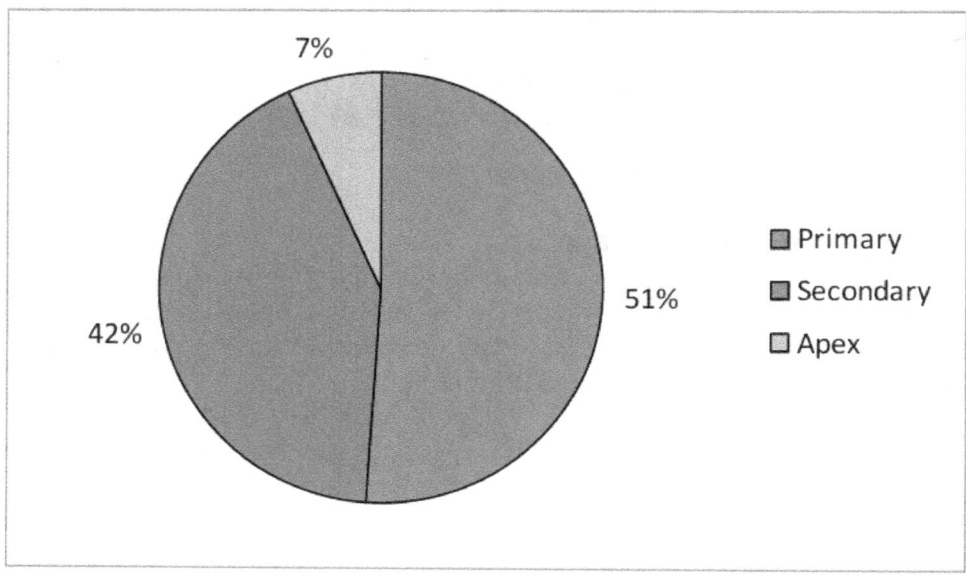

Figure 8. Relative biomass of fish consumer groups at Kalaupapa National Historical Park in 2008.

Top Ten Fish Species

In terms of density, the secondary consumer *Chromis vanderbilti* was by far the most abundant species found at Kalaupapa in 2008 with $34,592 \pm 183$ SE fish/km^2 x 1,000 documented (Table 2). It was more than eight times as abundant as the next two most common taxa in the park combined, the secondary consumer *Naso hexacanthus* and the primary consumer *Kyphosus* spp. The bulk of the biomass, however, was accounted for by these two species (Table 3). Each of these taxa accounted for more than twice the biomass as the third highest biomass species, the primary consumer *Acanthurus olivaceus* (437.7 ± 8.3 mt/km^2). Six of the top ten most abundant species by density were secondary consumers, while four were primary consumers (Table 2). In

10

comparison, the top ten most abundant species by biomass were composed of five primary consumers, four secondary consumers, and one apex predator (Table 3).

Table 2. Top ten fish species by density [(no./km^2) x 1000] at Kalaupapa National Historical Park in 2008. Common names are from Randall (1996).

Species	Common Name	Hawaiian Name	Consumer Group	Density [(no/km^2) x 1000]
Chromis vanderbilti	Blackfin Chromis	unknown	Secondary	34592
Naso hexacanthus	Sleek Unicornfish	kala lōlō, 'ōpelu kala	Secondary	2200
Kyphosus spp.	Rudderfish	nenue	Primary	1904
Thalassoma duperrey	Saddle Wrasse	hinālea lauwili	Secondary	1632
Acanthurus nigrofuscus	Brown Surgeonfish	mā'i'i'i	Primary	1616
Acanthurus leucopareius	Whitebar Surgeonfish	māikoiko	Primary	1520
Ctenochaetus strigosus	Goldring Surgeonfish	kole	Secondary	1328
Paracirrhites arcatus	Arc-eye Hawkfish	piliko'a	Secondary	1208
Chromis ovalis	Oval Chromis	unknown	Secondary	1032
Acanthurus triostegus	Convict Surgeonfish	manini	Primary	864

Table 3. Top ten fish species by biomass (mt/km^2) at Kalaupapa National Historical Park in 2008. Common names are from Randall (1996).

Species	Common Name	Hawaiian Name	Consumer Group	Biomass (mt/km^2)
Naso hexacanthus	Sleek Unicornfish	kala lōlō, 'ōpelu kala	Secondary	1211.08
Kyphosus spp.	Rudderfish	nenue	Primary	1029.71
Acanthurus olivaceus	Orangeband Surgeonfish	na'ena'e	Primary	437.66
Naso unicornis	Bluespine Unicornfish	kala	Primary	414.20
Bodianus bilunulatus	Hawaiian Hogfish	'a'awa	Secondary	306.87
Acanthurus leucopareius	Whitebar Surgeonfish	māikoiko	Primary	287.99
Acanthurus dussumieri	Eyestripe Surgeonfish	palani	Primary	258.11
Caranx melampygus	Bluefin Trevally	'ōmilu	Apex	252.99
Monotaxis grandoculis	Bigeye Emperor	mu	Secondary	197.73
Ctenochaetus strigosus	Goldring Surgeonfish	kole	Secondary	182.50

Trends of Fish Assemblage Characteristics

At the 15 fixed transects surveyed annually, mean fish species richness (24.5 ± 0.2 SE; Figure 9) remained relatively stable from 2006 to 2008. Mean fish density showed a slight decrease in 2007, although the level in 2008 (1,744.5 ± 295.3 fish/km^2 x 1,000) nearly returned to the 2006 level (1,904.5 ± 445.5 fish/km^2 x 1,000; Figure 10). Finally, like species richness, mean fish biomass (158.4 ± 6.1 SE mt/km^2; Figure 11) and mean fish diversity (2.00 ± 0.01 SE; Figure 12) remained relatively stable from 2006 to 2008.

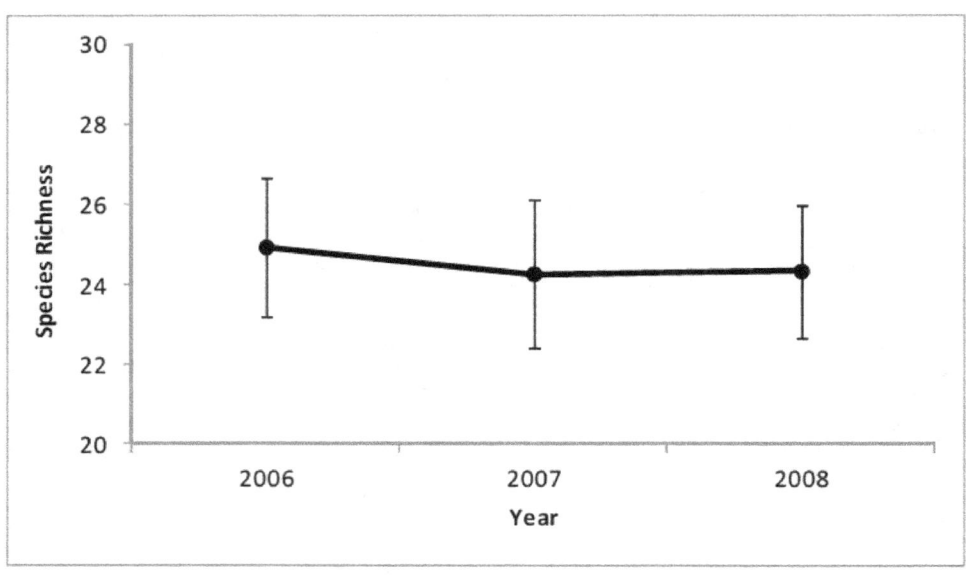

Figure 9. Fish species richness (no./125 m^2) at Kalaupapa National Historical Park from 2006-2008. Error bars are one standard error of the mean.

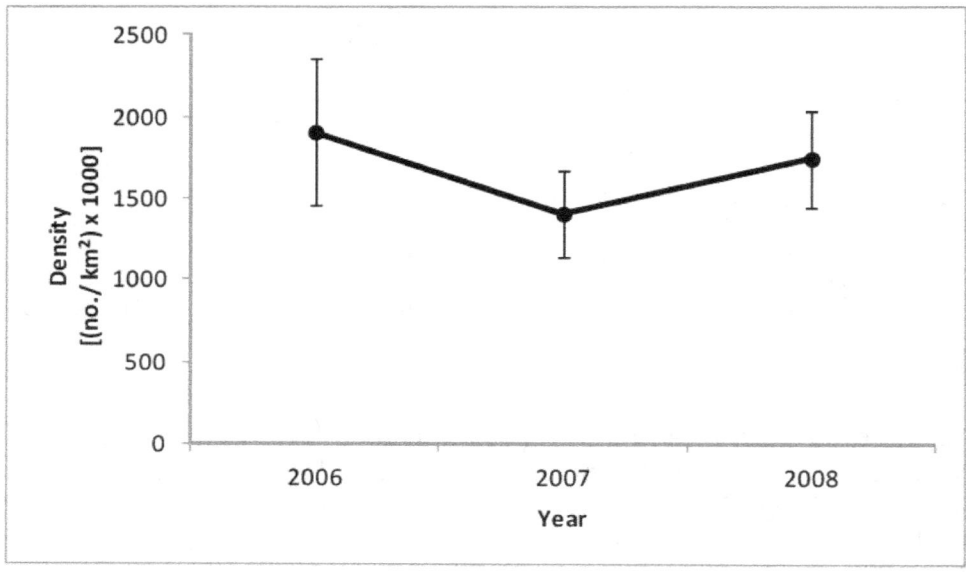

Figure 10. Fish density [(no./km^2) x 1000] at Kalaupapa National Historical Park from 2006-2008. Error bars are one standard error of the mean.

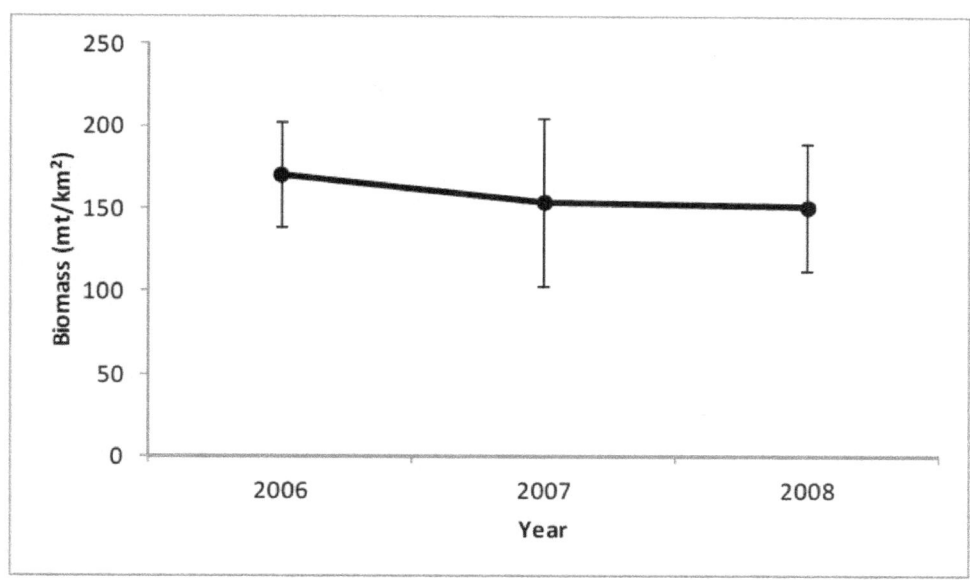

Figure 11. Fish biomass (mt/km^2) at Kalaupapa National Historical Park from 2006-2008. Error bars are one standard error of the mean.

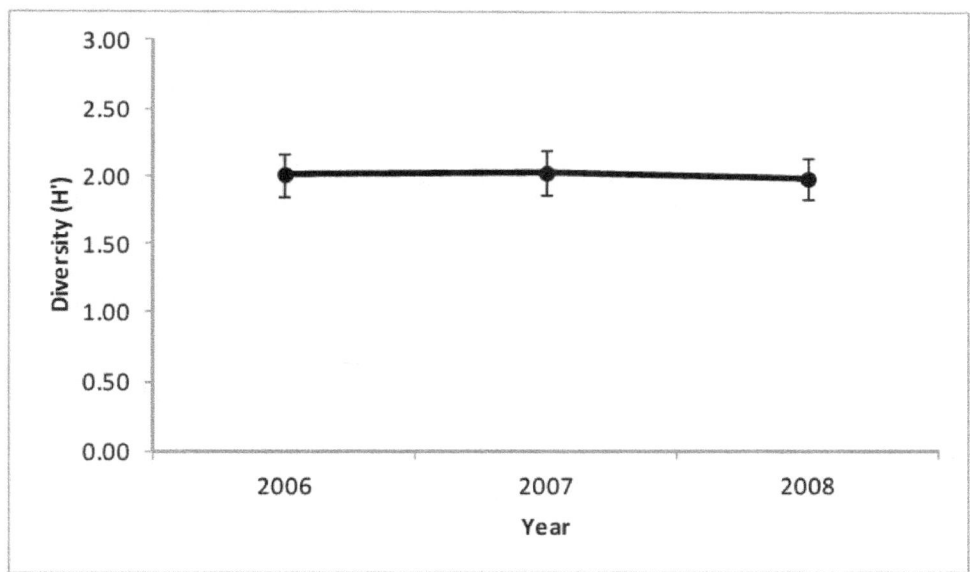

Figure 12. Fish diversity (H') at Kalaupapa National Historical Park from 2006-2008. Error bars are one standard error of the mean.

Discussion

No clear correlations were found among the distribution of fish species richness, density, biomass and diversity throughout Kalaupapa National Historical Park. Fish species richness was lowest on the western shore, and highest along the eastern shore, of the Kalaupapa peninsula (Figure 3). The lowest fish densities were found near the western boundary of the park and along the southwestern coast of the peninsula (Figure 4), while the highest densities were concentrated near the northern tip of the peninsula. The highest diversity values were concentrated near the western boundary of the park (Figure 6). In terms of biomass, one transect (temporary transect 10), located on the eastern coast of the peninsula, had more than twice the biomass observed at any other transect due to a large school (230 individuals) of *Naso hexacanthus*.

Secondary consumers accounted for 83% of the fish observed during 2008 (Figure 7). The most abundant fish species observed in Kalaupapa, the secondary consumer *Chromis vanderbilti*, was more than eight times as common as the next two most common taxa in the park combined (Table 2). The diminutive size of this species (up to about 7 cm; Hoover 2008), largely influences the relative density versus biomass of the trophic groups. While secondary consumers account for 83% of the individual fish observed (Figure 7), they make up just 42% of the biomass (Figure 8). In contrast, while primary consumers had a relative abundance of just 16% (Figure 7), they accounted for 51% of the biomass (Figure 8). This is due to the fact that several large primary consumers are quite common in Kalaupapa (Tables 2 & 3), including *Kyphosus* spp. (up to 60 cm), *Acanthurus olivaceus* (up to 30 cm), *Naso unicornis* (up to 69 cm), *and Acanthurus leucopareius* (up to 25 cm; sizes from Randall 1996).

Of particular ecological importance to the PACN parks are the apex predators. Worldwide, large apex predators have been on the decline with many, including sharks, disappearing at alarming rates (Worm et al. 2006). These (typically) large predators are important to the reef because their absence can cause dramatic shifts in the species composition and dominant taxa of a reef. At KALA, in 2008, apex predators accounted for just 1% of individual fish observed (Figure 7), but constituted 7% of the biomass (Figure 8). This relatively high apex predator biomass could be partly due to the light fishing pressure at Kalaupapa (Tom 2010).

At the 15 fixed transects surveyed annually, mean fish species richness (Figure 9), mean fish density (Figure 10), mean fish biomass (Figure 11), and mean fish diversity (Figure 12) remained relatively stable from 2006 to 2008, although density showed some variability with a slight decrease in 2007 and recovery in 2008. Further data collection and rigorous statistical analyses in subsequent reports will help us clarify the trends in Kalaupapa's fish populations.

15

Literature Cited

Atlantic and Gulf Rapid Reef Assessment (AGRRA). 2006. The AGRRA protocols. Available at http://www.agrra.org/method/methodhome.html (accessed 11 May 2010).

Beets, J., E. Brown, and A. Friedlander. 2010. Inventory of marine vertebrate species and fish-habitat utilization patterns in coastal waters off four national parks in Hawai'i. Pacific Cooperative Studies Unit Technical Report 168. University of Hawai'i at Mānoa, Department of Botany, Honolulu, Hawai'i.

Birkeland, C. 1997. Symbiosis, fisheries and economic development on coral reefs. Trends in Ecology and Evolution 12:364-367.

Bohnsack, J., and S. Bannerot. 1986. A stationary visual census technique for quantitatively assessing community structure of coral reef fishes. NOAA Technical Report NMFS 41, National Oceanic and Atmospheric Administration, Southeast Science Fisheries Center, Miami, Florida.

Brown, E., J. Beets, P. Brown, P. Craig, A. Friedlander, T. Jones, K. Kozar, M. Capone, L. Kramer, and L. Basch 2011. Marine fish monitoring protocol- Pacific Islands Network. Natural Resource Report NPS/PACN/NRR—2011/421. National Park Service, Fort Collins, Colorado.

Coles, S. L., L. Giuseffi, and M. Hutchinson. 2008. Assessment of species composition, diversity and biomass in marine habitats and sub-habitats around offshore islets in the main Hawaiian Islands. Bishop Museum Technical Report No. 39, Honolulu, Hawai'i.

Connell, J. H. 1978. Diversity in tropical rain forests and coral reefs. Science 199:1302-1310.

English, S., C. Wilkinson, and V. Baker. 1997. Survey manual for tropical marine resources, 2nd edition. Australian Institute of Marine Science, Townsville, Australia.

Friedlander, A. M., DeFelice, R. C., Parrish J. D., Frederick, J. L., 1997. Habitat resources and recreational fish population at Hanalei Bay, Kaua'i. Final Report to State of Hawai'i, Department of Land and Natural Resources, Division of Aquatic Resources, Honolulu, Hawai'i.

Friedlander, A. M., E. K. Brown, P. L. Jokiel, W. R. Smith, and S. K. Rodgers. 2003. Effects of habitat, wave exposure, and marine protected area status on coral reef fish assemblages in the Hawaiian archipelago. Coral Reefs 22:291-305.

Hill, J. and C. Wilkinson. 2004. Methods for ecological monitoring of coral reefs. Australian Institute of Marine Science, Townsville, Australia.

Hoover, J.P. 2008. The ultimate guide to Hawaiian reef fishes, sea turtles, dolphins, whales and seals. Mutual Publishing, Honolulu, Hawai'i.

Kulbicki, M., G. Mou Tham, P. Thollot, and L. Wantiez. 1993. Length-weight relationships of fish from the lagoon of New Caledonia. Naga, ICLARM Q. 16:26-29.

Randall, J.E. 1996. Shore fishes of Hawai'i. University of Hawai'i Press, Honolulu, Hawai'i.

Reef Environmental Education Foundation (REEF). 2010. Geographic zone report. Available at http://www.reef.org/db/reports/geo/haw/43040001 (accessed 7 May 2010).

Rogers, C. S., G. Garrison, R. Grober, A. M. Hillis, and M. A. Franke. 1994. Coral reef monitoring manual for the Caribbean and western Atlantic. National Park Service, Virgin Islands National Park, Central, U.S. Virgin Islands.

Samoilys, M. 1997. Manual for assessing fish stocks on Pacific coral reefs. Australian Centre for International Agricultural Research, Department of Primary Industries, Brisbane, Australia.

Sweatman, H., D. Bass, A. Cheal, G. Coleman, I. Miller, R. Ninio, K. Osborne, W. Oxley, D. Ryan, A. Thompson, and P. Tomkins. 1998. Long-term monitoring of the Great Barrier Reef. Australian Institute of Marine Science, Townsville, Australia.

Tom, S.K. 2011. An investigation of the cultural use and population characteristics of 'opihi (Mollusca: *Cellana* spp.) at Kalaupapa National Historical Park. Master's thesis. University of Hawai'i, Hilo, Hawai'i.

Worm, B., E. B. Barbier, N. Beaumont, J. E. Duffy, C. Folke, B. S. Halpern, J. B. C. Jackson, H. K. Lotze, F. Micheli, S. R. Palumbi, E. Sala, K. A. Selkoe, J. J. Stachowicz, and R. Watson. 2006. Impacts of biodiversity loss on ocean ecosystem services. Science 314:787-790.

Appendix A: Database Queries Used to Generate Reports

STATUS MAPS (for all transects):

	Data	Excel File	Columns in Excel File	Database Query
1.	Species richness	Fish Summary Status Maps	Sp Richness	qs_f021_Fish_Summary_by_Transect
2.	Density/abundance	Fish Summary Status Maps	Density (Num/km2)x1000	qs_f021_Fish_Summary_by_Transect
3.	Biomass	Fish Summary Status Maps	Biomass (mt/km2) *Note: mt=metric tons*	qs_f021_Fish_Summary_by_Transect
4.	Diversity	Fish Summary Status Maps	Div	qs_f021_Fish_Summary_by_Transect

TREND LINE GRAPHS (fixed transects only (combined); units the same as in status maps):

	Data	Excel File	Columns in Excel File	Database Query
1.	Species richness	Fish_SpRichness_Trends	All years	qs_fr041_Fish_Species_Richness_Trend
2.	Density/abundance	Fish_Density_Trends	All years	qs_fa041_Fish_Density_Trend
3.	Biomass	Fish_Biomass_Trends	All years	qs_fb041_Fish_Biomass_Trend
4.	Diversity	Fish_Diversity_Trends	All years	qs_fd041_Fish_Diversity_Trend

PIE CHARTS (for all transects combined):

	Data	Excel File	Columns in Excel File	Database Query
1.	Trophic composition by density	Fish_Trophic_Chart	Primary, Secondary, Apex	qs_ft001_Fish_Trophic_Abundance
2.	Trophic composition by biomass	Fish_Trophic_Chart	Primary, Secondary, Apex	qs_ft002_Fish_Trophic_Biomass

TABLES (for all transects combined):

	Data	Excel File	Columns in Excel File	Database Query
1.	Metadata	Metadata	All columns	qs_md001_Metadata_by_Transect
2.	Top ten species by density	Fish_Top_Ten_Density	TaxonName, SumOfNum_km2 x 1000, Consumer	qs_fa061_Fish_Top_Ten_Density
3.	Top Ten species by biomass	Fish_Top_Ten_Biomass	TaxonName, SumOfBio_mt/km2, Consumer	qs_fb061_Fish_Top_Ten_Biomass